"Adventures of The Googs"

Life Through a Kid's Eyes

Xavier (The Googs) Does and Tim (Grandpa) Roehl

To Bruce & Joyce -
Thank you for your support!

Go with God! †
Googs & Grandpa
Psalms 32:8 ☺

Copyright © 2023 by Xavier Does and Tim Roehl

All rights reserved. No part of this publication may be reproduced, distributed or transmitted in any form or by any means, without prior written permission.

Tim Roehl and Xavier Does
8582 Polk St NE
Blaine, MN 55434
www.fitflourish.com

A Note from Googs: These stories are based on my real-life adventures. Grandpa and I did change the names of some of the people in my stories.

Book Layout © 2014 BookDesignTemplates.com

Adventures of the Googs: Life Through a Kid's Eyes
Xavier Does and Tim Roehl -- 1st ed.
ISBN 9798865696353

Dedicated to:
My Family

"Life's an adventure, especially through a kid's eyes."

—Tim Roehl

What Others Are Saying About *"Adventures of The Googs"*

"*Adventures of The Googs: Life Through a Kid's Eyes* was a great collection of stories that our family truly enjoyed. These sweet stories and the discussion questions that follow each one create an opportunity for children (and adults) to connect and grow through everyday life lessons. Googs goes through many important moments in his stories, learning to be brave, practicing being a good teammate, learning the value of hard work, and many others. Each lesson is relatable and interesting to children and provides a clear pathway to have positive and impactful conversations."
- Hannah Jacobson
  Children and Family Ministry Director and Mother of 4

"A sweet retelling of life's lessons learned with family. You can almost feel like a part of the story and connect to the simple truth and lesson in each chapter."
- Pastors Ryan and Sarah Trosen
  Children and Youth Ministers
  Restore Church, Marshalltown, IA

"*Adventures of The Googs* does the sweetest job of reminding us to intentionally parent, guide, and engage meaningfully with our kids. These stories underscore the importance of being present with patient listening. They encourage children to have real moments and not stuff feelings away. They help us as parents make space, inviting kids to ask any and every type of question so they learn and grow. Most significantly, through each and every "adventure" a child encounters, there is ALWAYS an opportunity for us to point them to truth about their Creator, and the strength and peace that can only be found in their Savior."
- Barbara Kochendorfer, Children's Minister, Author
  ChristLIfe Church, Columbia Heights, MN

"We have had the privilege of sitting under Tim Roehl's ministry on various occasions over the past two decades. I (Bryan) also had the privilege of holding Xavier (The Googs) when he was just a few days old (His parents are dear friends from college). What we've enjoyed most about Tim's teaching over the years is that he always leaves you with a "What now?" section at the end of his messages, inviting us to apply ancient Biblical truth to MY life today. He takes Biblical narratives and makes them tangible experiences. We love that Tim and Xavier have taken this same approach with the stories in this book and the "Now for Your Adventure" sections. We especially appreciate how it helps me open up conversations with our own three daughters. In fact, we were able to immediately apply the lesson of "Googs Learns to Be a Good Teammate" with our oldest daughter Cecilia as she is just starting her first year of organized basketball with fifth-grade girls at her school. We look forward to unpacking these stories with each of our girls as they grow up and follow in the footsteps of The Googs. Thank you, Tim and Xavier! To see your cross-generational friendship unfold through these stories is truly a rare joy."
- Bryan and Molly Canny, Tutoring Center Directors, Bolivia Children's Ministry, Faith E Church, Billings, MT.

"From the best bait for fishing to teamwork on the basketball court and even losing baby teeth and questions about loved ones who passed away-- "Googs" and his Grandpa Tim have captured some of the life-changing questions kids ask their parents into a collection of short stories. After each story, kids are invited to have their own adventure as they can talk with their family what they learned from "Googs." We especially appreciated the kid-ified Christian concepts placed in the book to help introduce things like heaven, missions, and prayer to kids in language that even "Big Kids" can understand."
— Rev. Jason and Lora Campbell, Missionaries to Kids

Welcome to ...

Adventures of the Googs
Life Through a Kid's Eyes

Hi!

My name is Xavier, but my family calls me "Googies" or "The Googs" for short. I live with my dad, mom, brother Ian (his nickname is Bubs) and cousin T...and two kitties named Ivan and Bella. Right now, I am in the seventh grade.

My mommy likes to tell stories about when she was a little girl. She and my Auntie Elise ("Weef") liked going places with their daddy and mommy (Grandpa and Gigi). Sometimes things didn't go as planned...they would get lost or something didn't go right. Mommy remembers Grandpa saying, "Girls...we're having an adventure!" Somehow things would turn out all right. When Mommy tells me those stories, she always smiles. I decided that I want to go on adventures, too!

Grandpa tells stories and writes books. One day I said, "Grandpa...how about if you and I write a book together?" Grandpa smiled at me and replied, "That's a great idea, Googs! I'd love to do that. What would you like us to write about? I thought for a minute. "Me!" Grandpa smiled and nodded. "That sounds wonderful. How about if we write about your adventures? We can call it, "Adventures of The Googs: Life Lessons Through a Kid's Eyes."

I said, "That sounds great. So...can we write about my adventures, but also help kids learn more about God?" Grandpa nodded, "That's just what I had in mind, Googs! When we tell your adventures, we'll help kids look at their own adventures. Best of all, we can help kids your age learn more about how much Jesus loves them."

Then we both smiled at each other. We knew that's what we were supposed to do! The stories you are about to read are written by Grandpa and me... I want to tell you about my adventures...and you can learn more from your adventures, too!

The Goog's Adventures

1. Googs Learns to Be Brave..................................11
2. Googs Learns to Be a Good Teammate..............17
3. Googs Learns to Earn..23
4. Googs Takes Medicine.......................................29
5. Googs Talks with God..33
6. Googs and His Brother......................................39
7. Googs and the Tooth Fairy................................43
8. Googs Goes Fishing..49
9. Googs Is Tempted..57
10. Googs Goes to a Funeral..................................63
11. Googs Get Creative...71
12. Googs Looks Ahead..75

10 · GRANDPA AND GOOGS

ADVENTURE ONE

Googs Learns to Be Brave

Do you ever get scared?

I do. I get scared when I hear loud noises. Loud noises hurt my ears and I don't know what to do. That makes me even more scared. Sometimes I start yelling and try to run away from the loud noise.

What do you do when you get scared?

One time I got scared was when there were fireworks on the 4th of July. When other people were looking up in the sky and saying, "Ooh" and "Ahh", I was covering my ears and saying, "Ow!" and "It hurts!" Even when I went in the house, it was still too loud! Finally, my dad took me in our car for a ride so I couldn't hear those loud noises. I am grateful my dad knew what to do. My daddy loves me.

Not long ago, Mom, my brother and I went with Grandpa and Gigi to see a train museum. It was fun...at first. We had a man who knew all about trains walk around with us and tell us all about them. He was our guide. Grandpa said, "Listen close, Googs. It's fun to learn and this guy knows a lot."

Our guide told us all kinds of interesting things. We even got to walk through an old mail train car... they used to deliver people's letters from a train. Gigi's dad had been a mail carrier. I thought that was awesome.

Gigi told me that some people love trains. They read books about them and like to make their own model train run around the tracks they set up. She said my older cousin Cody has loved trains since he was my age.

Those trains were so big! I learned that people used to ride in trains before there were even cars. They even had little trains set up like a whole little town! Then our guide told us how trains talked to other trains...and to people in the towns they went through. He said every train had a whistle that would go, Toot, Toot! The train would make short whistles and long to send different messages. He said you could hear a train whistle from a long way away.

He also said each train had a loud bell and showed us one. He said, "Here's what it sounds like." He swung a little rope that made the bell move...and it went clang, CLANG! It was LOUD! Right away I put my hands over my ears. It was too loud! Maybe trains weren't so cool after all.

Finally, our guide said, "Now for the best part of your tour...you get to ride on a real train! It won't be a long ride and you'll have fun." He walked with us outside and pointed to a real train. "There's your train ride!" he said.

Wait, I thought. Is that train going to make loud noises? I turned to My mommy while I was still looking at our guide and said, "Does the train make loud noises?"

Our guide said, "Well, they might have a whistle."

That did it. I wasn't going on any train that made loud noises! "NO!" I yelled. "I'm not going!"

My mommy put her arm around me. "It will be all right, Googs," she said.

I pulled away from my mommy. "NO! I'm not going…it will be too loud." Everyone tried to get me to go—Mommy, my brother, Gigi, Grandpa—but I kept yelling "NO, NO, NO!"

Finally, Grandpa said, "You guys go ahead, I'll stay with Googs." Grandpa put his arm around me and walked me back inside. We sat down on a bench and I leaned my head on his shoulder.

"Googs," Grandpa said. "I get scared sometimes, too. It's part of life. But…we don't have to stay scared."

I leaned my head back and looked up at Grandpa. "How do you do that?" I asked.

Grandpa smiled down at me. "Well, first…it's OK to say we are scared. That's just being honest. Plus, the Lord knows it anyway."

I nodded my head. "Did you know that in the Bible there are 365 times where it says, 'Fear not...' or, 'Don't be afraid.' In many of those verses the Lord also says, 'I am with you.'"

I thought for a second. "That's one time for every day of a year!" I said.

Now Grandpa nodded. "That's right! The Lord knows we need His help when we are afraid, so we can tell Him. He won't be mad at us. But then there is something else we need to do."

"What's that, Grandpa?" I asked.

"I was hoping you'd ask that!" said Grandpa. "When we are scared, we can say, I'm scared...but I'm also brave! I can overcome my fear!" That's what I do...and the Lord helps me. You are a brave young man, Googs. I know you are scared, but I know you are also brave. What do you think?"

I snuggled in closer to Grandpa. *Am I brave?* I thought. Then I decided. "Yes, I am brave, Grandpa! But...will you be with me?"

Grandpa gave me a big Grandpa hug. "You bet! Shall we go ride that train?"

I nodded my head. Grandpa and I walked outside...and the train was just coming back. We met Mommy, brother, and Gigi as they got off. "Was it loud?" I asked.

"No, not at all! It was great!" said my brother.

Grandpa said, "Googs decided he would be brave and overcome his fear. He and I are going to ride the train. Do you want to come with us?" Everyone said yes. We all got on the train. It was great! Grandpa helped me get way up high on a seat in the caboose so I could see above everything. We had a great train ride.
We all got off the train. Everyone told me how proud they were of me.

"Time for a treat?" Grandpa said.

"Yes!" I yelled. "Let's go!"

Grandpa looked at me and smiled, his eyes twinkling. We both knew that I had learned something even more important than going on a train ride.

I am learning to be brave...even when I'm afraid.

Now for Your Adventure

1. What scares you? Share that with someone you love and talk with them about it.

2. Sometimes being afraid keeps us safe, like staying away from something too hot. Sometimes being scared holds us back from doing good things, like loud noises

do to me. Ask your mommy or daddy how to know the difference.

3. How can you be brave and overcome something you are afraid of? Talk to the Lord about your fear...then tell Him you want to be brave! He right there with you...and will help you!

ADVENTURE TWO

Googs Learns to Be a Good Teammate

Do you like to play any kind of sports?

I do...I like all kinds of sports! Football, baseball, Hot Wheels...but I *really* love basketball! I love watching basketball with my daddy on TV. I love playing basketball on my Xbox. I especially love playing basketball for real.

If you stood next to me, you might wonder why I like real basketball so much. You see, I'm kinda short. My dad's not real tall and my mom is shorter than him. Most people would say that means I wouldn't be very good at basketball.

But...Grandpa was a good basketball player and so is my dad. When I was pretty young and even shorter than I am now, my dad and Grandpa showed me how to shoot a basketball. At first, I couldn't even get the ball up to the rim...not even the net. But I kept trying!

It took a while, and I started getting the ball all the way up to the rim...and then the ball went in! I had scored a basket. It felt good! My daddy cheered. My mommy cheered. Brother cheered. I smiled real big! Then I called both Grandpas...they cheered for me, too!

After I made my first basket, I wanted to make more! Every time the ball went through the net, it was awesome. I imagined that I was like one of the players I watch on TV. I was the quick left-handed guard who could dribble down the court, make a smooth move and then shoot and score! I practiced and practiced! Even when it was too cold or rainy outside, I practiced on the little hoop I put on the door in my room. I practiced with a nerf basketball and my little basket. I practiced all the time!

When I was seven, my dad asked if I wanted to play on a team with other kids my age. I couldn't wait! Now I could show lots of people what a good basketball player I was! I was going to score LOTS of points!

At our first practice, I learned two things:
First, I found out I was the best shooter on our team. Second, I found out there is a lot more to playing basketball than just making baskets. Basketball teams

have five players, not one. I had only played by myself and for myself. Now I had to learn to play with a team and for the team.

I had a lot to learn. I already knew how to dribble and shoot and score. Now I needed to learn how to pass, play defense and work with my other teammates.

It was hard. I liked to shoot and score. I was good at it...better than my other teammates. But my dad taught me how to watch for who was open and pass the ball to them. He told me all that if I wanted to play, I'd have to be a good team player. He was serious. I listened.

I also had to learn to play defense. I had to learn to keep myself between the guy with the ball, the guy I was guarding and the basket. When Grandpa came to visit, he showed me how to do it...just like my daddy did! They were both good coaches!

My coach also taught us to encourage each other and cheer for each other. I was used to cheering for myself when I made a good play. Now I learned to cheer for my teammates when they made a good play. We learned to say, "Good play!" and "Way to go!" We gave high fives and fist bumps. We learned to point a finger that meant, "Good job!" at each other as we ran down the court. To be a good team, we had to learn how to play together. We had to learn how to cheer for each other. I learned that it wasn't all about me...it was about all of us doing our best.

The first couple of games we played, I led our team in scoring. But my coach reminded me that my passing and defense weren't so good. "Team, Googs," he told me. "Be a team player. Remember what team spells? T*E*A*M means, Together Everyone Accomplishes More.

Dad and Mommy came to all my games. My mom's a good cheerleader! She told me what Grandpa taught her when she was learning to play softball about my age.

"Grandpa taught me to remember three things. He said, 'Keep your eye on the ball, keep your head in the game...and listen to your coach." I tried to remember those three things, too.

I found that some of my teammates were better than me in different ways. Garrett is taller than me. He's a better rebounder. William plays better defense than me. Madden passes really well. But, when we each played our best at what we did best, we made a pretty good team. We were better together! Every game we played a little better. We won some and lost some...but we had fun. We were a team.

Grandpa and Gigi came for a visit to watch my brother Ian and I play basketball. Ian was on a team of older boys like him and I was on my team. Now it was Mommy, Gigi and Grandpa cheering for me! I wanted to play extra good that game. I tried real hard to pass the ball, watched for my teammates, played good defense and listened to my Coach. We won!

Finally, our basketball season was over. Daddy and I talked about what I'd learned. "You still led our team in scoring, Googs...but you also learned how to pass and play defense. You became a good team player! I'm proud of you."

I can't wait until the next basketball season. I'm going to practice dribbling and making different shots. I am also going to work on passing and defense. It's fun to be a good player...it's even better to be a good *team* player!

Wait until everyone sees me play...I mean, sees *us* play next season!

Now For Your Adventure!

1. What kind of sports do you like? If you don't like sports, what do you have fun doing?

2. What are you good at? Everyone's good at something. Be proud of that!

3. Remember, teams are not just about sports. Your family is a team. How can you be a better team player in your family?

ADVENTURE THREE

Googs Learns to Earn

Do you like to get presents?

I don't *like* to get presents...I *love* to get presents!

I love to get presents at Christmas.
I love to get presents on my birthday.
I love to get presents when my grandparents (both sides) visit me or I visit them.
I love to get presents on other special days...
I love to get presents on *any* day!
I'd love to get presents *every* day!

I love presents I can eat.
I love presents I can wear.
I love to get presents I can play with.
I love to get presents I can watch.
I love to get presents I can read.
I love to get presents I can collect.
I love to get *any* kind of present.
I love to get *every* kind of present.

One of the best things about being a kid is getting presents. It seems like all you have to do is ask your parents or grandparents or uncles, aunts or friends. Then you just remind them...and remind them and remind them. Usually that means I'll get that present. It's awesome being a kid!

One day I reminded my mom (again) about a present I wanted...a toy for my collection. She looked at me and said something I would have never expected. "Googs, if you want that toy, you'll have to work to earn it."

What?! Work? Earn? What in the world was my mom trying to tell me? I didn't know. So...I asked. "Mom, what do you mean have to *work* to earn that toy?"

Mom sat down with me and I knew it was going to be one of those "Mom wants to teach me something" moments. I waited.

"Googs, we love to give you presents on special days. We want you to learn our family value of being generous and grateful for what you receive from others."

"Mom, I am always grateful for the presents I get!" I said very seriously.

Mom nodded. "I'm always glad when you are grateful," she said. "But...part of life is learning to work for things we want. We can't just expect other people to give us everything. It's time for you to learn how to earn things you want by working for them. That's part of growing up."

Well, right then I was not too excited about growing up. Mom seemed to know what I was thinking... she always seems to know what I'm thinking. How do moms do that? Anyway, she smiled at me. "You may not like it at first, but you will really like earning things by your own hard work. You'll be proud of yourself...and your dad and I will proud of you, too."

"But...I don't wanna have to work! I just wanna get presents from others!" I was about to start getting mad and crying...that works sometimes to get what you want, you know.

Mom was already ahead of me. "I know, Googs, but this time you're going to learn to earn. How much does that toy cost?" I wasn't sure. Who cares what something costs when you can get it for free from somebody?

"I don't know," I said.

"Well, let's find out," said Mom. "Then you'll know how much money you have to earn in order to buy it."

We looked it up. I found out that my "free" present actually cost a *lot* of money. (At least it seemed like it to me.)

"I'll never be able to have earn that much money! I'll never get my toy!" I was not very happy.

Mom smiled. "You can do it!" she said. "It may seem like a lot, but little by little you'll earn enough to get your toy."

"How can I do that?" I wasn't convinced.

"Let's make a plan," Mom encouraged me. "I will pay you for doing some special chores around the house. You can ask other people if you can do something for them to earn money. If you work hard with a good attitude, you'll have enough money sooner than you think."

So, Mom and I made a plan. She listed some special chores I could do and how much she would pay me for them. "If you do your chores with a good attitude, I might even pay you a little more as a bonus." That sounded good to me!

So, I started doing chores. Every time I finished a chore, Mom marked it down...what I did and how much I earned. She kept my money for me. Mom's really good at taking care of money for our family.

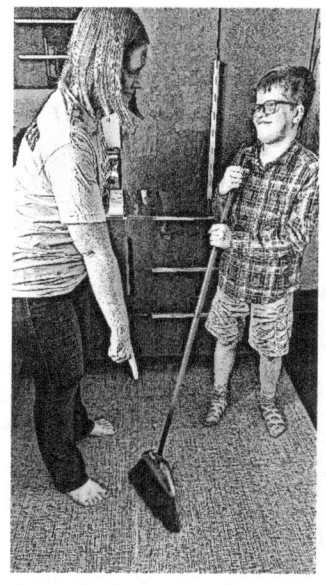

At first I wasn't real excited about having to work. But when Mom praised me and I saw my bank account growing, I started to like working. It was even fun sometimes!

I even earned money by doing special jobs for other people. When they told me I did a good job, it made me feel really good! One day after I finished a chore, Mom said the words I'd been waiting to hear. "Googs, you have enough money to buy your toy! How about we go to the store?"

I jumped up and down with happiness. "Yippee! Let's go!" I said on my way to the door. When we got to the checkout at the store, I saw she was a friend of ours from church. She was a mom, too. Mom gave me the money she'd been saving for me. I put it on the counter and smiled at the checkout lady. "I'm buying this toy with my own money! I earned it!"

The checkout lady smiled back at me. "Good for you...way to go!" Then I think she winked at Mom. Do all moms seem to know everything?

I held my new toy tight. I had earned it! With my own money! I smiled all the way home. Mom told me she was proud of me. That made me smile even more.

I was already thinking about the next thing I was going to earn.

Now for Your Adventure!

1. What are some of your favorite presents you've received from others?

2. Do you do chores at your house? What chores do you do?

3. What would you like to earn by working for it? It's fun...try it!

ADVENTURE FOUR

Googs Takes Medicine

Do you ever take medicine?

Sometimes when have a fever or my tummy hurts and I don't feel good, my mom gives me medicine to help me feel better. She says she always gives me medicine that's just right for my size. I'm glad Mom and Dad know how to give me the right medicine when I'm sick.

Do you know that sometimes you need special medicine that you take all the time?

When I was littler, sometimes I would have a hard time. I couldn't stay still, talked too much, fought with my brother a lot and got really mad sometimes. I did things I didn't want to do…it was frustrating for me and my family. Sometimes when I got frustrated, I would cry because I didn't know what else to do. My mom and dad love me and wanted to help me, so we went to see a doctor.

Have you ever had to go to a doctor? At first, I was a little nervous, but Dad and Mom said the doctor would be able to help us. That made me feel better because I trust Mom and Dad.

When we got to the doctor, she was real nice. That made me feel better. The doctor asked me questions. She asked my mom and Dad lots of questions, too. Dad and Mom talked with the doctor, using big words I couldn't understand, but I could tell they were trying to find out how to help me.

Then the doctor rolled her chair over to me so we could see each other eye-to-eye. I could tell she was serious, but her smile was kind. "Xavier (that's my real name, you know), our bodies are wonderful. We have bones and blood and lots of other parts that all need to work together so we can be healthy. Sometimes our bodies need extra help. That's why we take medicines when we don't feel well. Sometimes we need special medicines that we take all the time to make sure everything works together like it's supposed to work. I think we have a medicine that will help you feel better. You have a turbo charged brain and the medicine will help your brain slow down and work better for you. You'll take some medicine every morning. You will notice a big difference...a good difference."

I looked over at Mom and Dad. *What were they thinking? Was this all right with them?* They both smiled and nodded at me. Dad said, "We think this is a good idea, too. Let's try it and see what happens."

Well, if the doctor and my mom and my dad all thought taking special medicine would help, that was good with me.

So, we got the special medicine and I started taking it every day. Would the medicine really help me? I wasn't sure. But right away I noticed a difference. I could focus on school better. I didn't get mad so easily. I didn't fight with my brother as much. Dad and Mom noticed the difference, too. My whole family noticed the change...and we liked it!

Since then, the doctor has adjusted my medicine as I grow. I've also learned that some of my friends take special medicines, too. They don't all take the same medicine I do. They take the medicines their bodies need. I also learned that some of my friends don't take any special medicines because they don't need them. That's why doctors and other medical people are so important. They know how to help us.

Someday I may not need my special medicine anymore. Someday I may take other kinds of medicine. Like my mom says, "We'll see." For now, though, I'm grateful for special medicines that help our bodies work like God intended for them to work.

So that's the story of my special medicine. I'm going outside to play. See you again!

Now For Your Adventure

1. Have you ever had to go to the doctor? What was it like?

2. Have you or someone in your family ever had to take any special medicines? What did you notice when you did?

3. I'm really grateful for doctors and others who can help us when we are sick, aren't you? If you get a chance, tell them thank you.

ADVENTURE FIVE

Googs Talks to God

Did you know that you can talk to God? It's called prayer.

Did you know that God can talk to you? It's also part of prayer...it happens when we listen to Him.

Did you know that the Lord likes it when we talk with Him? Yup.

Did you know that you can talk with God anytime, anywhere about anything? It's true!

The answer to every one of those questions is YES! When I think about how awesome it is to be able to talk to God, I'm not sure whether to say, "Wow!" or "Awesome" or "Cool!" I think it's all three...and more! "WOW...AWESOME...COOL!"

You might ask me, "How do you know that, Googs? What's it like to talk with God?"

Well, those are good questions. First question first.

I know you can talk with God and God talks with us because our family does it all the time. For as long as I can remember, Dad and Mom have always talked about God, they talked with God, they listen when God talks to them and sometimes, they talk to God about my brother and me. Both my grandpas, Gigi, my other grandma and my uncles and aunts are the same way. We pray before our meals. We pray before we go to sleep. We pray when we travel. We pray about all kinds of things. My grandpa often says, "Let's pray about that" ...and we do! We thank the Lord when He answers our prayers.

It's not just *when* we pray...it's *how* we pray. Mom and Dad don't talk to God like He's far away and big and scary. They talk with God like I talk with them—they know God loves them and He is right there with them. They talk to Jesus like they trust Him. I hear them pray, "Nothing's too hard for You, Lord." They talk with the Lord, not like He's scary big, but He's *awesome* big!

Our family loves the Bible. Dad says it is God's Word...and He can talk to us through His Word. We read it and talk about it. Sometimes I hear Mom or Dad remind God of something He wrote in His word, especially His promises, as they pray.

I also learned about prayer from other people. Our friends pray, too. We pray at church. We kids pray in Sunday School. We pray when people get together at somebody's house. We pray for our families. We pray for each other. We pray for people who are sick or need help. We pray for our city. We pray for our schools. We pray for our nation. We pray for people who live far away who haven't heard about Jesus yet. Grandpa always prays for wisdom. Sometimes we just tell God how much we love Him and thank Him for how much Him loves us. Sometimes we tell God how wonderful He is in lots of different ways. Mom says that's called praise.

I've learned that people pray in different ways. Some are very respectful and quiet. Some cry when they talk to the Lord. Some pray loud prayers. Some pray looong prayers. Some use only a few words. Yet, they are all talking with the Lord. There's something good that happens when people talk to the Lord and listen to Him talk with them. It's hard for me to explain, but I can tell you being with God is really special. I know about prayer because we pray all the time.

What was your other question? Oh, yeah. You want to know what it's like when I talk with Jesus and Jesus talks with me. Well, it started when I was really little. When we would pray for our meals, Mom or Dad would say,

"Let's pray... put your hands together and bow your heads, boys." I knew we were doing something important. Sometimes I peeked to see if brother had his head down and hands folded. Sometimes he peeked, too! When Mom or Dad were down praying, they would say, "Amen." I would lift my head, smile and say, "A...men!" Mom and Dad would smile back and say "A...men!" too.

That's how I started praying. As I got a little older, Mom and Dad would ask me to pray! I wasn't sure what to say, but I just talked with Jesus about whatever came to my heart. Somehow, I knew He was listening and smiling at me. It felt good. I've been praying ever since... sometimes out loud, sometimes just quietly. I know Jesus can hear me even with no one else can.

I'm still a kid, but one thing I know is that Jesus loves kids like me and you! In my Kid's Bible there's a story about a bunch of kids who wanted to hang out with Jesus. I imagine that He picked them up in His big strong arms, hugged them tight to His heart, tossed them up in the air and then caught them, laughed with them and played with them. I know that He asked them what their names were and about their families. I know He taught them about His Father in words they could understand. That's the Jesus I know, too!

Some grouchy older people told the kids to leave Jesus alone and go away. But the Bible said that Jesus told the grouches to leave the kids alone...that He loved them! "Let the little ones come to Me," Jesus said. "You've got to have a heart like these children to understand what it's like in my Father's house. My Father loves those who just want to be with Him...who love Him no matter what and trust Him with everything."

What's it like when I talk with God and He talks with me?

When I'm scared, He answers me with His peace.

When I'm mad, He just holds me close. Sometimes He uses my mom or dad to do it.

When I do something bad, He lets me know. I can tell that He's sad.

When I ask Him to forgive me, He does. He speaks His love to me from His heart.

When I'm not sure what to do, I ask for His help. He gives me a thought that I know is His guidance.

When I do something good, I can feel His smile. It's like He is saying, "Way to go, Googs!"

When I'm worried about my friends or family, He lets me know that He is with them, too.

I can talk to Jesus anytime, anywhere about anything! Wow! Awesome! Cool!

You know what?
You can talk to Jesus like that, too.
Try it and see.

Now For Your Adventure

1. Who do you know that talks with God? What are you learning about prayer from them?

2. How often do you talk with God? Remember, He is always near and we can talk with Him anytime!

3. What would you like to talk with Jesus about right now? Go ahead and tell Him...and don't forget to listen to what He says back to you!

ADVENTURE SIX

Googs and His Brother

How many kids are in your family?

Some families I know only have one kid. Others have lots of kids! My Gigi liked a TV show that had 20 kids in the family! Wow!

There's two kids in our family. You already know me...the Googs. I have a brother, too. His nickname is Bubs. My brother is almost three years older than me. That makes him the *big* brother.

What's it like to have a big brother? Well, that can be a tough question to answer. I love my brother, I really do. But...sometimes he's well, annoying.

Sometimes he does stuff just to pester me. He will say things that I don't like. Other times he pokes me and it really bothers me. When I poke him back, it seems like I'm always the one who gets caught by my dad and Mom. When I say, "But he started it," sometimes they don't believe me. It's not fair!

Ok, I admit that I start things with Bubs sometimes. Then he's the one who complains!

Our mom and dad are pretty smart...no matter who started the problem, we both get in trouble! If I didn't know better, I'd say they did the same things when they were kids, too.

It's annoying when my big brother gets to do things that I can't do because he's older. Sometimes I tell my mom and dad, "That's not fair! I should get to do what he's doing, too!" They just smile at me and tell me to wait until I'm older. Then Bubs teases me because I'm the little brother. That makes things even worse! Harrumph!

Yup, my brother Bubs can really annoy me sometimes.

But...what he doesn't know is how much I look up to him and want to be like him.

My brother is really smart. He knows lots of things. He gets really good grades. He has a zillon Hot Wheels cars and knows the name of every one of them. He's a car expert! I watch what he does and try to do the same thing most of the time. Why do I do that? Hmmm...

that's a good question. Sometimes because he does things I want to do, too. Sometimes because I want to learn from him. Sometimes it's because some of my friends try to imitate their older brother or sister. The shortest answer is... because he's my brother, I guess.

But...I am starting to realize that as much as I love my brother, we are not the same. I like different things than him and he likes different things than me. He plays saxophone in band and I play trumpet...or maybe I'll try drums (if my mom will let me have drums in the house!). He likes to learn about the weather. I like to track the scores of my favorite teams.

Dad says God has a special plan for each of us. Even though we are from the same family and we both belong to God's family, God may have different plan for each of us. Someday we may even live far away from each other like my mom lives far away from her sister.

Even if we do live far away someday, Bubs will always be my brother and I'll always be his brother. That's never going to change. My mom says she used to squabble with her sister when they were little, but now they talk on the phone all the time. I can see how much they love each other. Dad is the same way with his brothers and sisters, too. I hope when we get older, we'll be like that.

Yup, my big brother still bugs me sometimes. Somedays he bugs me most of the time! But there's something very special about having a brother even when they are annoying.

Don't tell him, but I love my brother. I even want to be like him sometimes. I think I'll keep him.

What About Your Adventure?

1. How many kids are in your family? What number kid are you?

2. What do you like about your brother(s) and/or sister(s)? Tell them...they will appreciate it!

3. How are you different than your brother(s) and/or sister(s)? How do you feel about that?

4. Even when you annoy each other, always remember that no one else in the whole world gets to be your brother or sister. Love them...pray for them...and surprise them sometime by doing nice things for them!

ADVENTURE SEVEN

Googs and the Tooth Fairy

Have you ever lost something? Me, too.

Have you ever lost something you were supposed to lose? I bet you have…even when you didn't know it at the time.

That's what happened when I lost a tooth. Actually, I have lost many teeth…and I was supposed to lose them! Let me tell you about the adventure I had when I lost one of my teeth.

One night, I felt some pain in my mouth. I was very serious to find out where the pain was coming from. I put my hand on one of my teeth where I felt the pain…and the tooth wiggled!

When I realized that my pain was coming from a wiggly tooth, I raced downstairs to tell my grandma, who was visiting us.

"Grandma!" I said, "I have a wiggly tooth."

Grandma said something back to me that I never believed I would have to do to get that tooth out. She said, "That's one of your baby teeth, Googs. You are supposed to lose it so your adult teeth can grow in. You'll lose all those baby teeth one at a time. That tooth is pretty wiggly, so it will come out without too much trouble. Here's what to do: get some mouthwash and swirl it around in your mouth. It will ease the pain and make it easier to get that hurting tooth out."

"Ok," I said, but I wondered how mouthwash would help my tooth come out. I went in the bathroom and got a bottle of mouthwash off the shelf. Looking at it, I was curious. Would it really work? I unscrewed the cap as if there was a missing message inside the bottle. I didn't know how much I needed, so I just took a little sip from the bottle into my mouth. I swirled it around and spit out the mouthwash. Grandma was right...it did feel better!

A few minutes later, I took a paper towel and grabbed that tooth with it...and it came right out! It hardly hurt at all. Ta-da!

I showed my tooth to my grandma and told her the mouthwash worked just like she said it would. She smiled and nodded her head. I think she'd given the same advice before! Then I showed my tooth to my dad.

Do you know what I did next? Maybe you've done it, too if your mom and dad told you about the Tooth Fairy like they told me. They said that if I put my tooth under my pillow, when I woke up in the morning, the tooth

 would be gone, and the Tooth Fairy would trade me a dollar instead! You can be sure I put that tooth right where the Tooth Fairy was sure to find it!

In the morning, the first thing I did when I woke up was to check under my pillow. Can you guess what I saw? Yup...no tooth...and...one dollar!

When I ran downstairs to tell Dad, Mom and Grandma that the Tooth Fairy had left me a dollar, they looked at each other and smiled. Mom said, "The Tooth Fairy keeps getting more expensive." I wasn't sure what she meant by that. I was just happy to have a dollar.

Later I got to thinking about that tooth. Where did the Tooth Fairy take it? Where did the Tooth Fairy live? Was there a great big place where all the teeth children have lost from all over the world are stored? How does the Tooth Fairy know when every kid has lost a tooth in every home in every country every day? How many languages does the Tooth Fairy speak? How many kinds of money does the Tooth Fairy have to give every kid something in their own kind of money?

Wow...that Tooth Fairy must be pretty busy!

I asked my grandma all those questions. She laughed and told me I asked really good questions! "Googs," she said, "One day I'll answer your questions. Today, just enjoy that dollar and watch for your grown-up tooth to grow in where you lost your baby tooth."

Well, now I'm a little older. I still have some baby teeth I've got to lose. But I have figured one thing out...guess who really is the Tooth Fairy? It's my mom! I acted like I was asleep when I put a tooth under my pillow one time and waited to see what the Tooth Fairy really looked like. The Tooth Fairy is my mom!

The next morning, I told Grandma my big discovery. She nodded and smiled. She already knew! "Googs, guess who was your dad's tooth fairy when he was little?"

The answer came to me in just a second...my eyes got bigger and I said, "Ahhh..." out loud. "It was you, wasn't it, Grandma?"

"Yes, it was me. Every mommy and daddy get to be the Tooth Fairy for their kids. It's a fun part of being a parent. Someday you'll get to be the Tooth Fairy for your kids."

I guess I'm learning more things as I'm growing up... There are some things you have to leave behind so better things can replace them, like baby teeth and grown-up teeth...

The Tooth Fairy may just be a make-believe story, but it's a fun story for parents to tell their kids anyway...

Even if the Tooth Fairy isn't real, it's still great to trade a tooth for a dollar!

Now For Your Adventure...

1. Do you still have any baby teeth? What are some ways your parents (or even your grandma) have helped your teeth come out?

2. What stories have you figured out are just made up, but were still fun when you were younger?

3. There are things we lose when we are little, but there are better things to replace them! What are some lessons you are learning as you grow up?

ADVENTURE EIGHT

Googs Goes Fishing

Do you ever wonder what your grandpa and grandma did when they were kids?

They will be glad to tell you. It's not hard...all you've gotta do is ask them...and when you do, you better be ready to hear some stories! Grandpas and grandmas have lots of stories to tell about when they were kids. Sometimes they will even show you what they did when they were kids. That's happened to me more than once. Let me tell you about one of those times....

We were visiting my Aunt Elise and Uncle Tim at their house. They live in a little town where you can walk to lots of places. Grandpa and Gigi were with us, too. We always have fun when we're all together.

We decided to take a walk down to a place where a little river flowed over a dam and under a bridge. It was pretty. When we got there, we saw some people were fishing. Grandpa looked at them and I could tell he was pretty interested, so we walked over to them.

"Catching anything?" Grandpa smiled as he asked them.

"Not much!" They smiled back.

Grandpa and the fishermen started talking about fishing stuff...I didn't understand much of it, but it sure made Grandpa excited to talk about fishing. They talked about what kind of fish lived in the waters, what kind of bait was good, what color lures they liked to use, what time of day was the best time to fish and where was the best place to fish around there...and even more! Wow...I didn't know there was so much to learn about fishing!

Grandpa looked at my brother and me and said, "Boys, let's go fishing! I'll show you how to fish like my dad taught me."

I looked at my brother and he looked at me. We'd never been fishing before, so we weren't sure what we were getting ourselves into, but we said OK.

Grandpa found some fishing rods with reels on them and we walked to where there was a place that looked like the deck on a house, only it was over the water. When we looked over the railing, we could see some little fish swimming! Cool!

"Looks like some sunfish," Grandpa said. "We call them "sunnies". Want to see if we can catch a few?" Grandpa smiled at us. "You hold the rod and I'll put on the bait," he said.

When we saw what he put on the hook, we were surprised. What do you think he put on the hook?! You'll never guess! He put peanut butter on the hook!

"They'll like peanut butter," Grandpa said, winking at us. I had no idea that fish liked peanut butter.

We moved over to the railing and Grandpa helped us put our line with peanut butter on the hook down into the water a little bit. "Watch what happens," he whispered. Gigi was looking down into the water, too. She was just as curious as we were.

All of a sudden several of the little fish gathered around the peanut butter! Then then started to nibble on the peanut butter.

"Wow…." I heard myself saying. My line started to jerk as one of the little fish tried to swim away with the peanut butter on the hook.

"Pull up!" Grandpa said. He was trying to help us both at the same time.

We pulled up…but there was nothing on the hook. "Well, they got away…let's try it again" Grandpa said as he started putting on some more peanut butter. "If at first you don't succeed, try again."

We tried again…and this time when my line jerked and the little fish started to swim away, I pulled up…and the fish stayed on the hook!

"You caught one!" Grandpa yelled. "Way to go, Googs!" We pulled the fish over the railing…it was wiggling and squiggling all over the place! It made me a little scared.

"Want to touch it?" Grandpa held it so it wouldn't wriggle so much. I touched the fish with one finger. It was wet and cold and slimy! Yuck! Suddenly I wasn't sure I liked fishing at all.

"I don't want to fish anymore! I don't like fishing! Let's go back to the house!" No matter what Grandpa, Gigi or brother said to me, I just kept getting more upset.

"Ok...let's go home" Grandpa said. He gently took the little fish off the hook and put it back in the water. See? It's swimming away...the little fish is all right." He was trying to make me feel better, but it wasn't working.

When we got back to the house, Grandpa sat with me on the couch. "Googs, did you know that the first disciples who followed Jesus were fishermen? They probably started fishing when they were boys about your age."

"Really? I didn't know that." I said looking up at Grandpa's face. His eyes were looking at me that special way when I knew he was sharing something important with me.

"Yup...and they were probably a little scared when they tried fishing the first time, too. But they didn't give up. They kept trying until they got good at it."

"You mean...like if at first you don't succeed, try again?" I asked.

"Exactly! I know you will learn to like fishing, too. I'll be right with you to help you."

"Well...if you'll be with me, Grandpa, I'll try again."

Grandpa hugged me. "Good! We'll try again a little later."

Sure enough, after a little while we went back to the pier and tried fishing again. Same rod, same hook, same peanut butter...only this time when I caught a fish, I wasn't scared! We all clapped and cheered. I smiled a big smile. "I did it! I did it!" We all cheered some more. This time I helped Grandpa put the little fish back in the water. "Bye, little fish! Maybe I'll see you again sometime!" I waved as it swam away.

We celebrated with a treat back at the house. "I'm glad you like fishing," Grandpa said. "I'm also proud of you for trying again." We grinned at each other.

"Googs...did you know there's something I like even better than fishing for fish?"

"What's that?" I asked.

"Well, when Jesus called those fishermen to be his disciples, He told them that if they followed Him, He would teach them how to fish for people. He meant that we get to help other people want to become followers of Jesus, too. There's nothing better than seeing Jesus change people's lives. He pulls us out of the bad places of sin and puts us in a whole better life with Him. That's what I love to do! And...do you know what Jesus uses for bait?"

"Peanut butter?" I guessed.

Grandpa laughed and laughed. He clapped his hands and laughed until tears ran down his face. "Good guess, Googs...I guess He could use peanut butter, but they didn't have peanut butter in those days. Jesus uses His love, forgiveness and His power to help us. That's what He uses to catch our hearts...and when He catches our hearts, He changes our hearts to be like His. That's how He caught me. I'm so glad He did." Grandpa's face looked happy, content and grateful.

We were both quiet for a bit. "Grandpa, thanks for teaching me about fishing today. Thanks for being patient with me when I wanted to quit. Will you take me fishing again?"

Grandpa smiled and nodded. "You bet," he said.

"Grandpa, thanks for telling me about the fishermen who followed Jesus. I want to fish for people so they want to follow Him, too. Could you teach me how to fish like that?"

Grandpa smiled even bigger and he hugged me close. "Yes, Googs. Jesus and I would love to."

I wonder what kind of peanut butter I'll use.

Now For Your Adventure

1. Have you ever asked your grandparents what they did when they were kids? Ask them...you're going to hear some interesting stories!

2. Think of a time when you wanted to quit, but you tried again and succeeded. How did that make you feel? How can you help others who are thinking about giving up?

3. Have you ever told Jesus you want to follow Him as His disciple? If you haven't, ask Him with a humble heart to forgive you for your sins and to come into your life and change your heart. It's the most important decision you'll ever make! Then go share that with someone who is also following Jesus...they will be excited for you!

Happy fishing!

ADVENTURE NINE

Googs and Temptation

Have you ever felt like doing something you know you shouldn't do?

Me, too. Why is that?

How come even though I knew that Mom said to leave the candy alone because it was for something special that I still wanted that candy so much?

I mean...I knew right where it was. I could almost *taste* it in my mouth...yum-yum-yum!

But...Mom told me to leave the candy alone.

Then I heard a little voice, like it was talking in my ear. *Go ahead...take some of the candy. No one's going to know.*

Then I heard my mom's voice reminding me, "Leave this candy alone, Googs. It's for something special. You'll see later."

It felt like there was a tug of war going on inside me.

Take the candy.
No, leave the candy alone!

Back and forth the argument went. It felt like I was being pulled in different directions! It was not fun. The tugging back and forth kept going on. Then I noticed I was all alone. Dad and Mom had left to go do something. No one was around but me...

I got up and went over by the candy. I was just going over to look at it... Before I knew it, I was eating candy! Not just a piece or two...but lots of candy! All of a sudden, there was hardly any candy left in the bag. Oh, no!
I hid what was left of the candy, trying to cover it with another bag.

I went and sat back down in the living room, trying to act like nothing had happened. But...I knew. I knew I gave into the voice telling me to take the candy. I knew it was wrong, but I did I anyway. I felt miserable.
In a little while, Dad and Mom got home. I tried to act like nothing was wrong, but inside my tummy was upset. I decided I better go up to bed. Maybe they wouldn't notice...

But they did. Mom came around the corner with Dad right beside her. They didn't look very happy.

Mom was holding the candy bag. It was almost empty. "Googs, did you eat the candy?" Mom was asking in that voice that meant she already knew the answer.

"No! I didn't!" I knew I was lying, but I still tried to deny what I did. That made me
feel even worse. Mom and Dad sat down next to me. Dad put his arm around me, "Googs, what happened?" My dad was not happy with me.

I started to cry. Then I told them everything...about how good the candy looked and how good I knew it would taste. I told them about hearing a voice telling me to take the candy. I told them about how I could hear Mom's voice. I told them about how it felt like I was being pulled in two directions. I told them about how I took the candy...ate it...tried to hide it.

"I'm sorry. I don't know what happened." I just sat looking at the floor. Somehow, once I told them the truth, I felt better. But I knew I was still in trouble.

I thought Mom and Dad would be mad at me. "Googs, look at us," Dad said. I looked up at them slowly.

"Googs, we're disappointed in you. But we are glad you told us the truth," Mom said.

"We could give you a punishment for what you did," Dad said. "But...we can see you are already feeling bad about this. You will still have to use your own money to pay to replace the candy." I nodded my head. That made sense.

"You can learn a very important lesson from this...if you're willing." Dad was looking at me with a serious look in his eyes. "Are you willing?"

"Yes," I answered. "I'm willing."

"You gave in to temptation," Mom said. "Do you know what that means?"

"I think so...but I'm not really sure," I replied.

Dad said, "Googs, temptation is when you feel a tug to do something you know is wrong. It happens to everyone."

"Even you and Mom? Grandpa and Gigi?" I asked.

"Everyone gets tempted. God loves us and He wants to give us good things. His way is always the best way! But if we're selfish or listen to the voice that tells us to disobey God, it messes things up. When we choose the wrong way, it's a sin. It hurts God's heart...and your mom and dad's hearts, too."

"Ouch," I said. "I don't want to hurt you...or God."

"Good," said Mom. "We don't want that either. Even when we do wrong, God still loves us. Even when you do wrong, we still love you...and Jesus still loves you."

"You can always come to Jesus for forgiveness when you give in to temptation," Dad said. "We forgive you because you were honest and said you were sorry. But...you don't need to give in when temptation comes."

"Thanks for forgiving me," I said. "My heart feels so much better. But I don't want to let temptation win. How do I not give in?"

"It's not always easy," said Dad. "We can't beat temptation by ourselves. We need the Lord's help. Jesus is stronger than temptation. We can go to Him for help when we are tempted. He promises He will."

"How do you know that?" I asked.

"He promises to always be with us," said Mom. "His Word has lots of promises."

"Here's one of my favorites," said Dad. "It's from First Corinthians 13:10: "Any temptation you face will be nothing new. But God is faithful, and He will not let you be tempted beyond what you can handle. But He always provides a way of escape so that you will be able to endure and keep moving forward."

"I understand," I said. "When temptation comes knocking at my door, I will ask Jesus to answer it for me!"

Dad laughed. "That's right, Googs! Let Jesus answer the door!" We all hugged each other...it felt like Jesus was hugging all of us and it sure felt good.

I laid in my bed thinking before I fell asleep that night. What a day. I had really messed up. But I had learned a lot. *"Jesus, I don't want to mess up...please help me,"* I prayed.

As I closed my eyes, I was sure I felt Him smile.

Now For Your Adventure

1. Have you ever felt like Googs felt when he was being tempted to take the candy? What was that like for you?

2. What did you learn about temptation?

3. What did you learn that will help you when temptation comes knocking at your door?

ADVENTURE TEN

Googs Goes to a Funeral

Have you ever come home and had the feeling that something wasn't right?

I got home from school one day and it was really quiet. My mom was sitting on the couch. She looked sad.

"Mom, what's the matter?" I asked. "You look sad."

"I am sad, Googs. It's a sad day...and a happy day at the same time."

"What do you mean?" I wasn't sure what she meant.

"Come sit with me," Mom said. I came over and sat by her. She turned to look at me and took my hand. "Your grandpa's daddy... your great grandpa Buzz...died today. That's why it's a sad day. I'm going to miss him."

Mom's eyes looked like she was going to cry. I felt like Mom needed a hug, so I hugged her close. For a minute, we didn't say anything. My Great Grandpa was pretty old and he lived far away from us. I had only been able to see him about once a year. I could remember sitting on his lap for pictures with Grandpa, Mommy and brother. When he smiled at me, his eyes twinkled like Grandpa's when he looks at me. He didn't say a lot, but his twinkling eyes and smile told me that he loved me.

"I'm sad too, Mom." Even though we were both sad, I felt better to be sad together with Mom. Then I looked up at Mom again. I was a little confused. "You said it was also a happy day, Mom. Why did you say that?"

Mom smiled at me and her sad look went away. "It's a happy day because Grandpa isn't sick anymore. He is in heaven now and he has a brand-new body that won't ever get sick again. Best of all, he is with Jesus now."

I'm just a kid, so this was too much to understand all at once. Grandpa Buzz had died. That was sad. But he wasn't sick anymore. That was good. He had a new body...what did that mean? He was with Jesus...that was good. How did that all fit together? I wanted to ask more questions, but wasn't quite sure what to ask, so I just hugged Mom.

In a couple days, our family made the trip to Grandpa and Gigi's house. My mom's sister Auntie Elise, Uncle Tim and my little cousin Simon were there, too. It felt good to be all together. I heard Gigi tell Mom, "Family needs to be together at times like this." They hugged each other. I love my family.

Grandpa picked me up and gave me a great big hug and tousled my hair like always. When he put me down, I looked up at him. "Grandpa, are you Okay? Are you sad? I'm sorry your daddy died." Grandpa bent down so he could look me right in the eyes. He smiled at me with that "I love you" smile.

"Yes, Googs, I am sad. I love my dad and I am sad because I can't see him and talk to him like I always have. But I'm also happy because he's not sick anymore. He's in heaven with Jesus and I know I'll get to see him again." That was almost the same thing Mom had told me! I still had questions, though. Maybe Grandpa could help me understand.

A little while later, Grandpa and I were sitting together outside on their deck. Grandpa looked over at me. "Googs, thanks for asking how I am feeling. How are you doing? Are you okay?"

It felt good to have someone ask me how I was doing. Sometimes kids get forgotten when the adults are all busy with other things. "Well...I'm kinda confused, Grandpa. I'm trying to understand everything, but it's hard."

"Like what, Googs? What are you wondering about?"

"Well...Grandpa Buzz died. So, he's not here with us anymore. That's sad. But Mom said he's got a new body that will never get sick anymore. Where's his old body? Where did the new body come from? He's in heaven with Jesus, but we will get to see him again. That's good. But how does that happen?" My questions seemed to tumble out all at once.

Grandpa nodded as I asked my questions. He was quiet for a minute and I could tell he was thinking. "Those are good questions, Googs. I asked the same kind of questions when I was your age. Can I share some things that have helped me to understand?" I nodded yes and waited.

"God made us in a special way. He made us into two parts. Part of us is like a house we live in…that's our physical body. The other part of us is a part we can't see, but it's even more special. That part of us lives forever…that's our spirit. Our spirit lives in our body. Your body is like the house you live in. Does that make sense?"

I nodded. "I think so…"

"Good…but there's more. Stay with me," said Grandpa. "Our bodies can get sick. They can get old. They don't last forever. So, someday we have to leave them behind. It's like moving out of our house."

"You mean like when we moved from Yakima to Marshalltown? We moved out of our old house into a new house." I was starting to understand.

"That's right!" Grandpa said. "When we die, it's only our physical body. We will move out of our old house.

It's sad for those who love us because we don't live in our physical body anymore. But it's very happy for us..." "Wait, Grandpa. What happens to our old house?" I asked.

Grandpa nodded again. "Good question. Well, we don't need it anymore, yet people want to take time to be sad together and share special memories about the person. So, in our culture we often have what is called a funeral or a celebration of life. Sometimes they dress up the body in a special way so people feel like they can say good-bye. Sometimes they don't have the body, but they have lots of pictures and things to help people remember. After the funeral we put the body...the old house that's not lived in anymore—in a place where we can always go visit and remember. Last month, your uncles and I decided to lay your Grandpa Buzz's old house to rest next to your Great Grandma. But we are celebrating his life at his funeral tomorrow." Grandpa smiled a quiet smile. "My mom and dad are back together again. What a joyful reunion they must have had!" Now Grandpa's eyes looked like he might cry. I could tell he missed them both.

"There's still more, Googs. Are you ready to hear the happy side answers to your questions?" "You bet!" I leaned forward. "When we move out of our old house, our spirit is still living. Your great grandpa and grandma love Jesus very much. They gave their hearts to Him to be their Savior. They were trusting God's promise in the Bible that says we get to spend forever in the special place God made for us to be with Him in heaven."

That's where we get our new body?" I asked.

"That's right! God gives us a new body that never gets old or gets sick. Someday I'll go there...Gigi will go there...our whole family will be together there!" "Is that because we've all asked Jesus to be our Savior?" I asked. "Yes," said Grandpa. "One of my favorite places in the Bible is in John 14 when Jesus was talking to His disciples before He went to the Cross. He told them He was going to His Father's House in Heaven but He would come again and bring them home with Him. Thomas was a disciple who always had questions. Thomas told Jesus he didn't know the way to Heaven and asked how he could know the way. Jesus told him--and us—the best news we can ever hear. He said, 'I am the way, the truth and the life. No one comes to the Father but through Me."

"Googs, God loves us so much that He sent Jesus to earth and gave His life for us so we could make our home with Him in heaven."

I was quiet. Thinking. Then, like pieces of a puzzle coming together, it began to make sense. "Ohhh...I think I understand, Grandpa. Grandpa Buzz is still alive, but he's moved out of his old house. He's home in Heaven with Jesus in His Father's House. He's got a new body...a new house to live in! Tomorrow we will be sad because Grandpa Buzz won't be with us here anymore, but we'll be happy because we get to remember lots of good things about Grandpa Buzz."

"Googs, you are pretty wise for your age." Grandpa said. "I think you are ready for the funeral now." The next day, our whole family was together with our uncles, aunts, cousins and lots of other people who loved

Grandpa Buzz. Everything happened just like Grandpa told me it would. Some people cried. Some told stories. Sometimes we laughed. Afterwards I was thinking about Grandpa Buzz. I wondered what he thought about the gathering with everyone talking about him...and Jesus.

I looked up and thought about him in his new body, happy with Jesus. I smiled.

You know what? I couldn't see them, but I got a real happy feeling that Grandpa Buzz and Jesus were smiling back at me.

Now for Your Adventure

1. It can be hard for kids to understand what happens when someone dies. How many of Googs' questions are questions you may have?

2. Who do you talk to when you have questions about things you don't understand?

3. What do you think about life and death now?

ADVENTURE ELEVEN

Googs Gets Creative

What are you good at?

Everyone's good at something.

I'll tell you something I'm good at…creativity! I use my creativity all the time! I use it when I'm writing. I use it when I'm drawing. I use it when I find ways to track the stats of my favorite sports teams. I'm even using creativity right now! I'm glad the Lord gave me the gift of creativity.

What do I mean when I say creative? Well, to me it means seeing normal things in new ways. Or coming up with new ideas that haven't been tried before. You know what I mean? Well, sometimes you just have to see it to understand it.

So, here's some ways I've been creative. I've made my own tracks for my marbles to roll down and around and around. I created my own sports team for a video game. But…sometimes my creativity can get me in trouble. Let me tell you the story…

It was a cold, cold, day. I was up to my regular business being the Googiest Googs I could be. How, you ask? Well, I had only one sock on! Sometimes I get really good ideas when I'm wearing only one sock. I had just watched a football game on TV. Well, because it was cold, I couldn't go outside and play. I like watching football. I like playing football, but it was too cold to go outside and play football. And yet...I still wanted to play football. What could I do?

Guess what happened? I got an idea! A creative idea! What if I could play football...inside?

I know what you are thinking...use a nerf football, tackle my brother, knock over a couch, break a lamp.

Nope...I've already done those things. My brother and I got in trouble that time and we didn't want to have Dad and Mom give us extra chores again. No way! I needed a different idea.

All of a sudden...I got an idea! A creative idea! A Googs idea! What do you think my idea was? Wanna guess? Well, it's on a board, it will have a winner and families can play it together.

What is it? It's a board game! But...not just a regular board game...I would create a board game about the USA! How would I do that? Well, first I needed a map of our country. Wait! I had one a couple years ago.

"Mom!" I called. "Do you remember where my map of the USA is?" Did you know my mom has Super Mom powers? She knew right where it was!

I took my map and started thinking about how people could play my new game. I thought and thought and thought some more...and pretty soon it was time for bed. I decided to act like a bear and go into hibernation until the next day. I slept like a bear, too. Mom said she could hear me snoring all the way downstairs!

The next day I got to work on my game again, still with only one sock on. My Googie creative skills kept working and my game was coming together.

It was ready for a test run. I went and showed it to my dad. He loves games like I do. Together we tried out the game. Dad had some good suggestions and helped me write down the rules of the game so they were easy to understand. Then we had Mom look it over...she had some good suggestions, too. We made a good team.

We test-played the game some more...and finally I felt like we were ready. We printed out the rules, put all the pieces together in a box...I was really excited. Googs the Great Game Maker!

Then I thought of one more thing...we needed to protect the game map and all the pieces. Mom said, "Let's laminate them." "Laminate them? What in the cheesy taco sandwich does that mean?" I asked.

Mom smiled, "A laminator will make your game map and pieces safe inside of plastic. But...we don't have a laminator." Then she got an excited look on her face. "Wait! I know what we'll do! We'll put the map, directions in plastic sleeves and put them in a binder!"

That's what we did. My Googs game was a success! We all went out for ice cream to celebrate.

Now I know you are wondering where you can get my game...well, we just made the one edition that we play at home.

Besides, I've already got some new ideas. My Googie creativity God gave me just keeps on working!

Now for Your Adventure

1. What are you good at?

2. How do you use the special gifts God has given you?

3. Try something new today just for fun. You'll be glad you did!

ADVENTURE TWELVE

Googs Looks Ahead

Do you know what you want to be when you grow up?

Me neither. Well, maybe I do...kinda.
I know there's some things I like to do.
I know there's things I like to watch others do.
But...I'm not sure if those things are what I want to do...or I'm supposed to do when I grow up.

You know what I mean?

Sometimes people ask me what I want to be when I grow up.

Sometimes I think about what I want to do when I grow up.

Sometimes I wonder if God has a plan for me.

Everyone in our family believes that He does.

Still, I wonder. So...I decided to ask some grown-ups if they knew what they would do when they were my age.

First, I asked my mom. She said, "I wanted to be a cashier at the grocery store." Then she smiled. "Even then, I wanted to help people with their money. That's what I do now." I nodded my head and thought *Hmmm...interesting.*

Then I asked Dad. "I wanted to be a sports broadcaster like the guys I watched on TV. I didn't become a broadcaster full time, but I get to help broadcast high school games now." I smiled, because sometimes Dad lets me help him.

Next, I asked my Gigi. "I didn't have any idea what I wanted to do when I grew up. It was in college that God called me to be a pastor's wife. That's what I get to do with your grandpa!"

I asked my Uncle TMo. "I wanted to be an astronaut or a firefighter. Lots of boys my age were the same way."

My Auntie Weef told me, "I wanted to be a lot of things when I was your age!"

All these answers were very interesting...and all were different.

Finally, I asked Grandpa. "Well Googs," he said, " Let me tell you my story. When I was your age, I wanted to be a sports broadcaster.

"Like my dad?" I asked.

"Yes, like your dad," Grandpa said. "My mom would come in my bedroom and I would be broadcasting hockey games in my sleep! I thought broadcasting games and sports scores would be great.

But God had other plans...better plans! When I was in high school I gave my heart to Jesus and He called me to be a pastor. I realized that He wanted me to broadcast the Best News anyone could ever hear--how much He loves us and wants us to be His children. That was better than telling people about scores of games everyone would forget. When people meet Jesus, we never forget what He does for us. I am so grateful I got to do what God called me to do!"

Grandpa smiled at me. "Guess what? During college I didn't play basketball for one year. I got to broadcast some of the games instead! So, I did get to be a broadcaster for a little while. It was a like a special gift from the Lord."

"Grandpa," I said, "I've been asking our family that same question. Everyone had a different answer. What am I supposed to do?"

Grandpa smiled at me again. "That's a good question, Googs. Here's some things to think about...

"First, God loves you very much.

"Then, look for some of His clues now...think about things you like to do...things that God can use to bless others.

"Remember, you can always count on His promises. One of my favorites is in Jeremiah 29:11 *"I know the plans I have for you, says the Lord...plans for good and not for evil...plans to give you hope and a future."* God always gives His best to those who leave the choice up to Him. Always!

"So...keep your heart open to the Lord. He will let know His good plan for you at just the right time. Whatever it is, it will be wonderful. We're all praying for you and believe in you!"

I nodded my head. Grandpa's words made me feel good inside. I knew what he was saying was true. If I didn't know what I was supposed to do now, I could wait. At the right time, the Lord would tell me. That was good enough for me. "That sounds good, Grandpa! I want God's best!"

"Good...just you wait and see," said Grandpa. "Until then, just keep living our family motto..."Remember?"

"Of course!" I shouted.

We said it together,

"Have fun, do your best...let Jesus shine through you!"

Now For Your Adventure

1. At this point in your life, what do you want to be when you grow up?

2. What are some clues you have about what God might want to you become?

3. Have you ever asked God what His purpose is for your life? If not, how about asking Him now. Tell Him you want His best and you'll leave the choice up to Him. Until then, how about sharing our family motto: "Have fun, do your best...let Jesus shine through you!"

FIT&FLOURISH

<u>From the Googs</u>: *"Do you know why I wanted to write a book with my Grandpa? It's because the Lord sends him all over the world to help people follow Jesus and train leaders who want others to follow Jesus, too. Here's some information I know you'll enjoy…"*

Our Calling: *"Leading leaders to discovery, clarity and destiny for the sake of eternity."*

Fit: This is where I belong.

Flourish: Lord, this is what You made me for!

Our A*C*T*S Framework for Ministry

<u>**A**ssessing</u> leaders, teams, churches and ministries so they can fit and flourish.

<u>**C**oaching</u> and training coaches worldwide.

<u>**T**raining/**T**eambuilding</u> for Kingdom impact.

<u>**S**piritual/ **S**trategic</u>: Supernatural/Intentional!

www.FitFlourish.com

Made in the USA
Monee, IL
19 November 2023